Go Away, Molly!

Shoo Rayner

Illustrated by Jon Stuart

OXFORD

In this story

Max

Molly

It was Saturday and Max woke up early. It was raining outside.
"I'm going to stay in bed and read my new comic," he said.
Molly wanted to play.

She jumped on Max's bed.
"Go away, Molly!" said Max.
"I'm trying to read my comic."

Molly still wanted to play.
She pulled the cover off his bed.
"No, Molly! Go and play on your
own," said Max.

Max read his comic as he ate breakfast.
"Will you play with me?" asked Molly.

"No, Molly! Eat your breakfast,"
said Max.
Molly still wanted to play.

Max went back to his bedroom.
"I know how to get away from Molly," said Max. "I could hide in my toy ship."
He pushed the button on his watch.

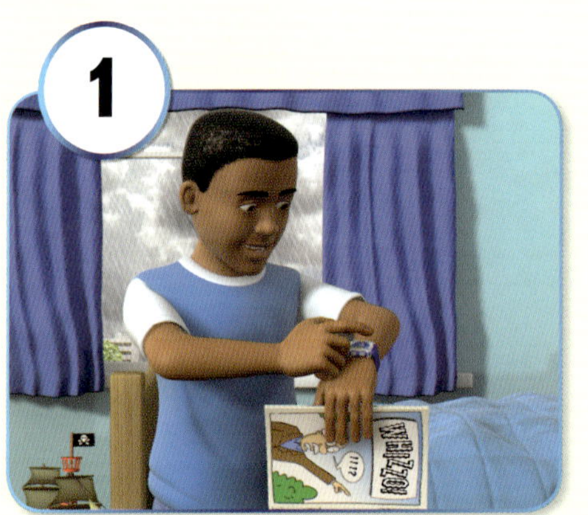

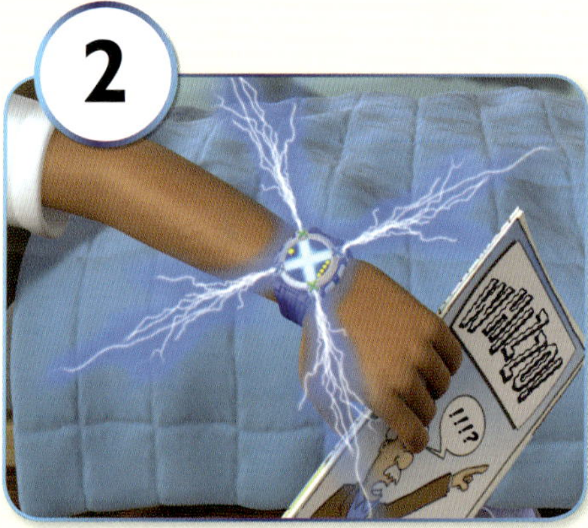

"Now I can read my comic at last!"
he said.

Molly went into Max's room to play.
She picked up his toy ship.

Suddenly the ship shook and Max slipped across the deck.

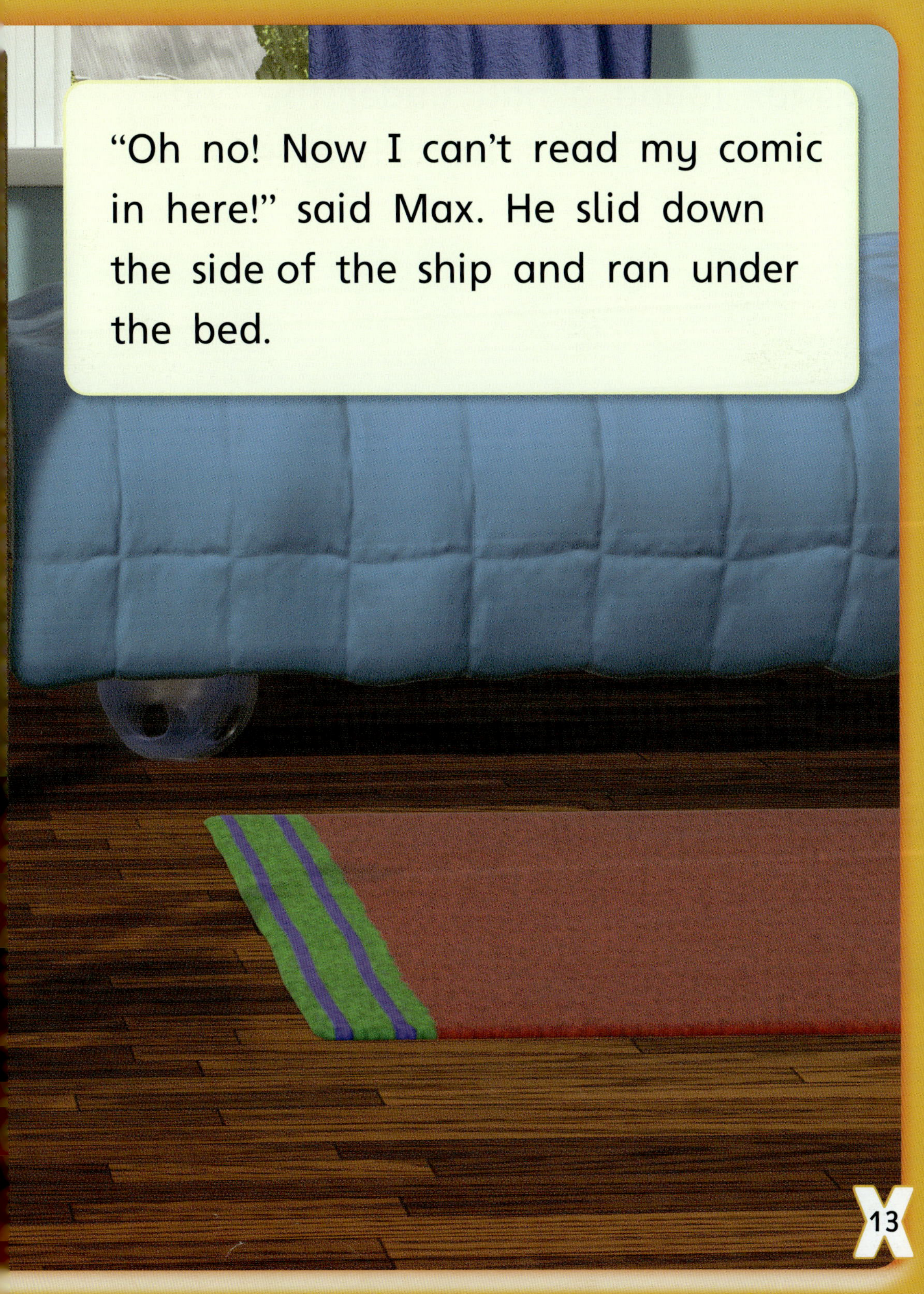

"Oh no! Now I can't read my comic in here!" said Max. He slid down the side of the ship and ran under the bed.

Max found a ball under the bed.
"I know," said Max. "I'll hide in there."

It was dark under the bed.
"I can't read my comic in here,"
said Max.
Slowly, he rolled the ball out from
under the bed.

Molly saw the ball rolling. She wanted to play with it!

Max started to run! Molly chased
the ball.

Max ran and the ball rolled out of
his room. It rolled along the hall.

Then it bounced down the stairs!

The ball landed with a bump.

Max rolled out of the ball and hid just in time. Molly picked up the ball and ran off.

Max pushed the button on his watch.

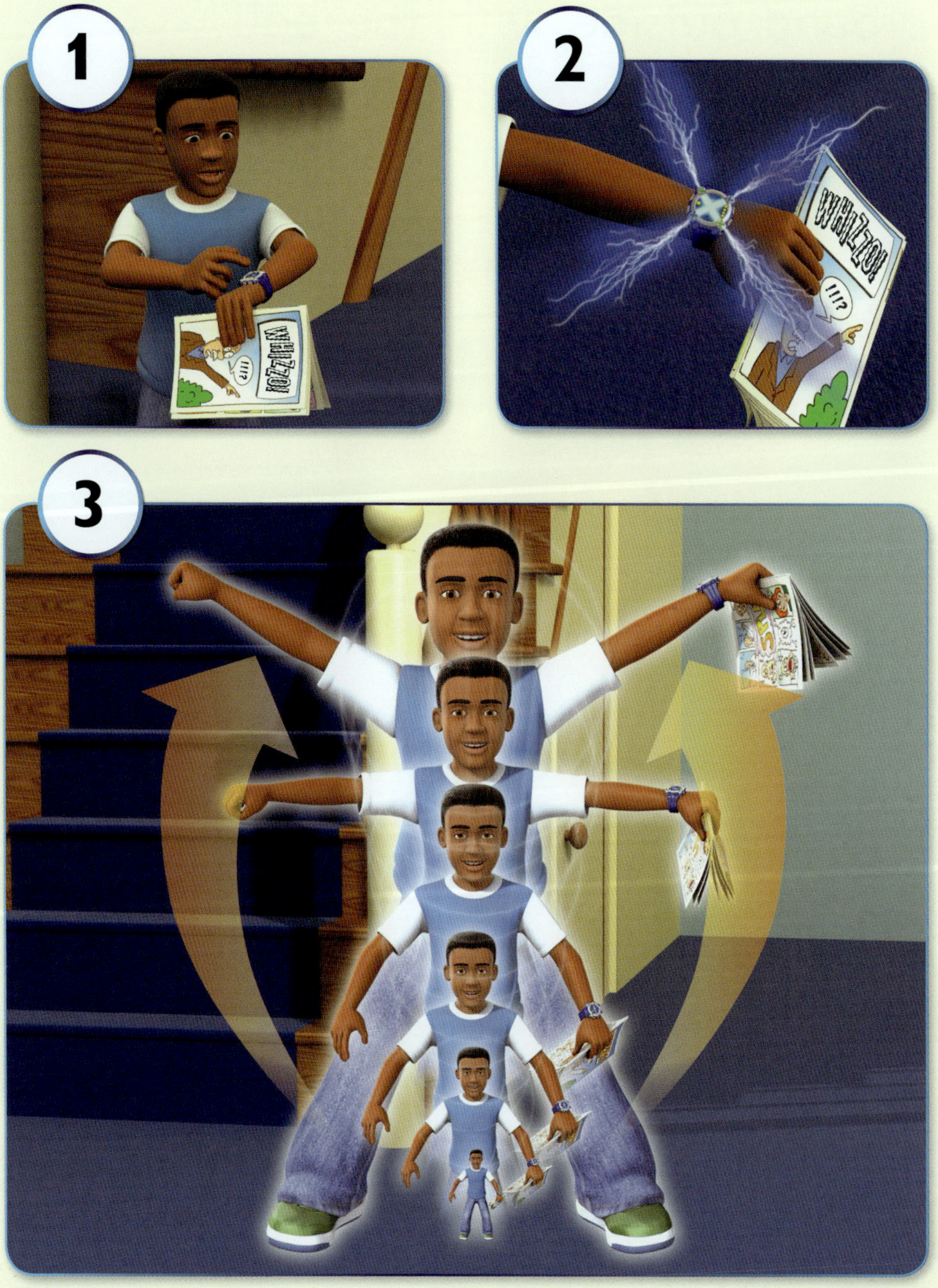

The rain had stopped and Molly ran
around outside with the ball.
"At last, I can read my comic!"
said Max.

"There you are!" called Molly.
"Will you come and play with me?"

Find out more

Read about an alien invasion ...

... and a bug invasion in a classroom!